Lil' Bean Goes Fishing

Lil' Bean's Adventures, Book 1

Shelia Hilbert "Bean"

ISBN 979-8-89243-027-2 (hardcover)
ISBN 979-8-89243-028-9 (digital)

Copyright © 2024 by Shelia Hilbert "Bean"

All rights reserved. No part of this publication may be reproduced, distributed, or transmitted in any form or by any means, including photocopying, recording, or other electronic or mechanical methods without the prior written permission of the publisher. For permission requests, solicit the publisher via the address below.

Christian Faith Publishing
832 Park Avenue
Meadville, PA 16335
www.christianfaithpublishing.com

Printed in the United States of America

Another lesson lil' bean learned from Dad was that you don't need money to eat or enjoy nature. When she was just a little seed, Dad taught lil' bean how to fish. Before she went fishing, Dad taught her about safety first.

When you go fishing, even if you don't get in the water or know how to swim, you need to wear a lifejacket. That way, if you fall in or near the water, you will float like a rubber ducky. This is also important if you decide to take a pet with you. Did you know they make life jackets for animals?

Dad told lil' bean that besides a life jacket, you need a fishing pole and bait. Dad's favorite bait was wiggly squirmy worms! You have to be very careful not to lose your bait so you can catch lots of fish. And remember to always take pictures of what you catch.

Another important thing I learned from Dad about going fishing is to make sure to pack plenty of food. Fishing takes a lot of patience and energy. One of lil' bean's favorite memories was having picnics with dad on a fishing break.

Some of our favorite things to pack on picnics were sandwiches, fruit, cheese and crackers, homemade lemonade or iced tea, and, if we were lucky, cookies for dessert. Our picnic fishing breaks were very special to lil' bean and Dad because we spent time talking, fishing, and gathering dinner for the family.

Come learn with lil' bean! Some of the fish Dad and lil' bean caught were catfish, bass, and trout. Have you heard of those fish?

Lil' bean shared something she likes to do that does not cost a lot of money. What is something you like to do or would like to do that costs little and brings you joy?

To my dad

    He taught lil' bean so much, and she wants to share those lessons with you! Dad taught me to be kind, always count my blessings, and stay positive even when things seem tough.

About the Author

Shelia Ann Hilbert is a proud coal miner's daughter. Shelia attended Ripley High School and graduated in 1981. She also graduated with her associate's degree in liberal arts and sciences from West Virginia University Parkersburg. Shelia has worked for the past twenty years at Renal Consultants PLLC, providing medical services. Her hobbies include writing children's books and animals, completing all kinds of charity work benefiting others, and all things Christmas!

Printed in the USA
CPSIA information can be obtained
at www.ICGtesting.com
CBHW061354250824
13581CB00011B/168

9 798892 430272